Maggy's Flower

A Division of The McGraw·Hill Companies

Columbus, Ohio

www.sra4kids.com

SRA/McGraw-Hill

A Division of The **McGraw·Hill** *Companies*

Maggy is a brown cow.

Maggy is big and powerful.
She is the most powerful cow in town.

Maggy plows.
The farmer's pals are amazed
at how well Maggy plows.

Maggy sees a lonely flower.
Maggy frowns. Maggy scowls.

Maggy stops her plow.

Maggy is allowed to keep her flower.
The flower makes Maggy happy, and when
Maggy is happy, she plows.